Raccoon

Karen Cline-Tardiff

Esperanza Publishing Edinburg, TX 78542

Book Cover Artist: Karen Cline-Tardiff

ISBN: 979-8-218-98523-3

"Night comes slower in the summer" Karen Cline-Tardiff writes in her new chapbook, *Raccoon*, which details the adventures of a modern family and the sharpening of their lives as they attempt to capture a wild creature. Stylistically inventive, filled with humor and light word play, Cline-Tardiff delves into what it means to look at what is wild and unpredictable. Her topic: the furry being who is probably watching us at this very moment; waiting and wondering what will happen next. Cline-Tardiff takes us on a fascinating tour of her dwelling. More! More! More!"

- Susan Kay Anderson, author of *Mezzanine*

"Set in the most ordinary of circumstances, with clear and succinct language, these poems are a meditation on how humans interact with the natural world."

- Su Zi

"Charge into *Raccoon*, where Karen Tardiff weaves a masterful narrative masking itself in the form of a serial poem - telling the existential struggle of woman versus the untamed force of nature. Karen Tardiff has metaphorically set the trap, loaded her frontier rifle, and put on her Davy Crockett raccoon cap in preparation for a new battle of the Alamo. Through evocative language and vivid imagery, Raccoon delves deep into the heart of suburban life, exploring the clash between humanity and the wild. This epic battle is fought along the themes of suburban encroachment and food scarcity—a visceral exploration of our innate connection to the natural world and the lengths we'll go to protect what's ours."

- Yrik-Max Valentonis, author of *120 Days of Gomorrah*, *Cranium Theatre*, and *Short Stories Without Provocation*

Once upon a time during the early days of Covid, we awoke to find our trash all over the yard. Blown here and there. In the garden, against the chicken coop, in the field across the way. There was only one culprit to blame. It being In the Time of Covid, this was high excitement. I diligently kept track of everything we tried to get rid of the pestering nighttime varmint. My husband regaled my daughter and I with the story of the marshmallow stealing creature when it awoke him and his best friend on their last 5-day float trip. Not a human in sight for days, but that little rascal somehow knew where the good stuff was hidden. We tried all kinds of ways to bind and lock our trash to keep him out, but to no avail. His opposable thumbs were smarter than we were, it seemed. So it was time for a trap. Once the ol' fellar was caught in the trap, the second half of the saga began. Our daughter, ever tender-hearted, didn't want us to kill it, just relocate it. We knew our captive, and his whole crew, would be back if we didn't take decisive action. I'm not sure if we made the right decision, but once it was over, it began again. Was it the same masked bandit or one of his crew? We'll never know. One thing is for sure, though. Ever since I finally turned the saga into this little book before you, raccoons have been popping up everywhere I look. Cute guys with striped tails at the bookstore in the form of bobbleheads, stuffed and adorned with crystals and magic at the hippie store a few towns over, even sneaking around the back door of our new home. And now, you have a Raccoon of your very own. Enjoy the show!

Karen Cline-Tardiff, 2024

1. The Raccoon

Little paw feet –
  Big appetite –

At night we would tuck our
trash into bins, hoping the
bungee cords would keep out
the nighttime visitors.

Quiet –
  Stealthy thieves –

Morning would prove we were
no match against the wily
raccoons who decimated the
plastic bags and strewn our
offal across the yard, laid us
bare for all the neighbors.

2. Hunger

16 million children struggle with hunger each year.

50% of all produce in the United States is thrown away.

About 1 in 5 children go hungry at some point during the year.

Wasted food is the biggest occupant of American landfills.

1 in 7 people in the United States face hunger every day.

30-40% of the food supply in the United States is wasted.

The average family of four discards nearly $1,600 of food annually.

Food insecurity is a topic of concern in the United States, caused not by food scarcity but poverty.

When schools close in the summer about 18 million children lose access to food.

218.9 pounds of food waste per person was reported in 2010.

A raccoon will eat up to 5 pounds of food in one night.

3. The Plan

We wanted the smelliest, most
enticing rancid food from the
back of the fridge, forgotten
food to be used
as an offering to
our nighttime
God of Discarded Waste.

We baited the trap and slept
snugly, secure in our
assumption the raccoon would
crash in and take the bait.

4. Brisket

"Only Texans and Jews understand brisket." Anthony Bourdain

Pounds of beef, a veritable slab,
rubbed in salt and pepper,
slapped around a lot.

It went into the black metal smoker,
on top of the diamond grates,
ubiquitous sights in Texas.

Tending the brisket was more
sacrosanct than going to church, may
God strike me dead if I'm lying.

Tending that brisket was like holy
communion, time and prayers
spent in smokey reverence.

The perfect red ring appears
as we slice into it, juicy fat
seeping through the meat.

We fight for the burnt ends,
a caramelized Eucharist.

5. The Bait

We tried tuna, the pouches
that wafted the smell of
anything but fresh sea.

We pulled the chili with nice
fuzzy mold into the plans for
bait.

Leftover lasagna seemed
to entice in the garbage
can, but not the trap.

We sacrificed a slice of
perfectly smoked brisket,
and the trap set.

We knew the power of
the right bait, and
no-sauce-needed beef.

6. Best Laid Plans
"The best laid plans of mice and men often go awry." Robert Burns

There are no raccoons in Scotland.

Or rather:
There are no raccoons native to Scotland.

Robert Burns never walked the Highlands,
bekilted, and encountered the putrid smell
of rotten meat salvaged from the bin.

Ayrshire was never host to these
nighttime denizens; but had Robert
encountered the bandit stealing from
barn to coop, perhaps he would not have
made love to Elizabeth, forced instead to
turn from poetry and romance to a life of
engineering traps.

Mouse traps are not effective against raccoons.

Or rather:
The better mouse traps are not meant for raccoons.

Robert would have turned his fancy
to ropes, levers, pulleys, and wires
instead of verse and histrionic songs.

Bully for us, the raccoon did not arrive in Scotland
until March of 2016. It was sighted in the
Highlands near Robert's old haunts.

There are no raccoons in Scotland.

Or rather:
The raccoon remained hidden in Scotland until suppertime.

7. Jailbreak

The trap was set.
       Baited.
We waited with
       Bated breath.

The night light
       Gleamed.
We awoke with
       Glee in our throats.

We put on our robes.
       Excited.
We stole outside to the trap.
       The raccoon exited.

The back of the trap?
       Sprung.
The escape hatch?
       Spring rain rusted.

8. DIY

Videos of how to build a better raccoon trap, Google video search response

"3 Ways to Build a Raccoon Trap" wikihow.com

"Easy DIY Raccoon Trap Step-by-Step" Survival Sullivan

"DIY Raccoon Trap! IT WORKED!" YouTube

"DIY Never Fail Raccoon Bait Easy and Cheap to Make" YouTube

"DIY Never Fail Raccoon Bait Easy and Cheap to Make" domyown.com

"How to Build a Raccoon Trap" HowStuffWorks.com

"5 Trapping Baits Nest-Raiding Raccoons Can't Resist" Realtree Camo

"Screw it, I'll build a better trap myself" My husband

9. DIY – Redux

The salt water and sun rendered the
metal springs useless.

The garage was scoured for
WD-40, JB Weld, Duct tape,
extra wire, a random spring, 2
bent nails, wrench, hammer,
Greased Lightning, used oil,
wire brush, Rust Out, and rags.

The raccoon didn't know what
kind of odds & ends junk
hoarder he was dealing with.

10. Trapping

"The sleek-furred fox and the elegantly spotted leopard ... can't seem to escape the disaster of nets and traps." Zhuangzi, 4th Century BCE

Animals may be trapped for a variety of purposes.

Early neolithic hunters created
crude traps for capturing wild
animals so they had enough food.

In the early days of the colonization of
the Americas, the fur trade provided
winter clothing for many settlers and
opened trade among the colonizers and
the colonized Indigenous peoples. And
led to the near extinction of certain
fur-bearing mammals.

In modern times, animals are frequently
trapped to prevent and minimize
damage to personal property and to
prevent the slaughter of livestock and
other preferred animals and pets.

Tonight, we trap for pest control:
the raccoon.

11. Wait

Night comes slower in the summer.

Cicada keen in the hours
between it-might-be dusk
and the-streetlights-are-on night.

We sat on the porch and
watched the grasshoppers
in the field leap into their
nighttime beds of grass.

Our daughter chased the
dog across the field adjacent
to our field, laughing as she
wrapped her arms around
her licking prey.

The scent of salt water
from the bay wafted
across the fields and
lulled us into our
nighttime routine.

Check the trap.

Set the trap.

Position the bait.

Wait.

12. Algebra

The Egyptians gifted us with many things:
community banking
fountain pens
battering rams
postal systems
horse stables
cloth sails
paved roads
the 24-hour day

13. Tilt

Summer days seem longer. The
earth tilts and rotates and spins
us around the sun. Some days
we get dizzy with the motion.

Some days we sit in one spot
and let the world tilt around us.

Our side of the earth just a
little more sunny, our patch
of green earth a little warmer,
our sun scattering all over us.

We wonder if the raccoon has
found a nest with a sunlit view.

14.

Cries went up
  across the land

He's been caught!!

Eyes flashing
  Teeth gnashing

Our warrior spirit declared
  across the lands:

Put his head on
  a stake as a warning
  to the other raccoons!!

We rallied around
  the metal cage

He hissed and
  clawed at us

We were brave
  in our security

Ding dong – He's Caught!!
  He's Caught!!
    He's Caught!!

15.

Our children are born full of love and empathy. They understand things about the world we have forgotten. My daughter's heart is full of innocence and she loves every living creature, sees the need for mosquitoes and only swats them away, refuses to crush them, while I gleefully kill any blood-sucker that comes near. She doesn't like it, this killing. Can't comprehend the glee, refuses to participate. She, too, has been frustrated by our nocturnal trash destroyer. She didn't participate in the baiting of the trap but tiptoed into the carport every morning to see if the troublesome raccoon had been caught. As we gathered round the cage she asked us "where will we let him go?"

16. Prisoner of War

According to Britannica, a
POW is any person
captured or interned by a
belligerent power during
war.

In early history, there
were no prisoners,
only captured; dead
or enslaved the only
outcomes.

As history progressed,
prisoners were treated
as property, a coin or
piece of paper of the
same value, tradable,
chattel.

De jure billi ac pacis
advocated for the
exchange or ransom
of prisoners of war.

History evolved again to
champion the prisoner
as human, just removed
from war.

There is no Geneva Conference
on the correct way to treat
belligerent raccoons, held
prisoner by victors of this war.

17.

We still haven't killed the raccoon.

At this point it would
 seem more humane

He's been in the metal trap
 for three days now,
 still hissing, still
 trying to claw his
 way to freedom

My husband floats the
idea of sneaking outside
in the dead of night,
putting a bullet in it's
head, dumping it in the
field for the vultures.

We end up sleeping through the night.

18.

"Shop our wide variety of .22 long rifle and other rimfire ammunition for plinking and small game hunting." Midway USA website

The purpose of ammo is
to project a force against
a selected target.

The effect is almost always,
but not always, lethal.

Ammo comes in a wide
variety of sizes and
types, so it's easy to find
the perfect ammo for
that impossible instance
when you need to kill a
raccoon but you can't
let your daughter hear
the shot and you're
having second thoughts
and maybe you're not as
hardened as you used to
be.

We have ammo for that.

19. Sunbathing

Sunbathing in a cage Back
on the ground Legs in the
air At first I thought "4
days. It only takes 4 days to
starve a raccoon." Then it
adjusted,

ensuring the tan was even,
despite the square cage lines.

20. Ouroboros

The deed is done.

It never happens
like we think it will.

The lid was popped off
the bin and Styrofoam
stained with leftover
lasagna is littering the
front yard.

The only thing left
to do is bait the
trap again.

Karen Cline-Tardiff has been writing as long as she could hold a pen. She is known for her uncensored views and her work mirrors her convictions. As the founder and Editor-in-Chief of Gnashing Teeth Publishing, she is committed to sharing work from diverse voices. Karen writes poetry and flash fiction, which has appeared in several different anthologies and journals, online and in print. When she can't find poetry somewhere, she puts it there.

www.ingramcontent.com/pod-product-compliance
Lightning Source LLC
Chambersburg PA
CBHW022351040426
42449CB00006B/831